THEY DIED TOO YOUNG

KURT COBAIN

BY
Andrew Gracie

||| •PARRAGON• |||

This edition first published by Parragon Books Ltd in 1995

Produced by
Magpie Books Ltd, London

Copyright © Parragon Book Service Ltd 1995
Unit 13–17, Avonbridge Trading Estate
Atlantic Road
Avonmouth
Bristol BS11 9QD

Illustrations courtesy of: Rex Features

ISBN 0-75250-720-6

A copy of the British Library Cataloguing in Publication
Data is available from the British Library.

Typeset by Hewer Text Composition Services, Edinburgh
Printed in Singapore by Printlink International Co.

THEY DIED TOO YOUNG
Kurt Cobain

On Tuesday, 5 April 1994, Kurt Cobain blew his head off with a shotgun. The body was discovered on 8 April. The police had to use fingerprints to make a positive I.D.; dental records were no use.

As the news spread, the story took on echoes of other violent celebrity deaths. Like Jackie Kennedy returning in a blood stained coat from Dallas,

Courtney Love, Kurt's wife, was inter-
viewed on MTV wearing the jeans,
socks and trainers her husband had been
wearing when he shot himself. The
comparison is not idle. As with J.F.
Kennedy, members of the slacker generation would remember where they
were when Kurt Cobain shot himself.
Through his music he had become an
icon, a symbol for the young of their
politics and aspirations. Kurt could not
cope with this elevation to messiah.

He made this clear in the suicide note
found beside his body. 'I haven't felt the
excitement of listening to music along
with really writing something for years
now. I feel guilty beyond words about
these things. The fact is I can't fool you.
It simply isn't fair to you or to me. The

worst crime I could think of would be to put people off by faking it, by pretending I am having 100 per cent fun. Sometimes I feel as if I should have a punch-in time clock before I walk on stage. I still can't get out the frustration, the guilt and the empathy I have for everybody. There's good in all of us and I simply love people too much. So much that it makes me feel too fucking sad. Too sad, a little sensitive, unappreciative, Pisces, Jesus, man.'

Having painted this paradox of the rock star who did not want to be a rock star, at the same time he conformed to all rock star expectations. The note finished 'So remember It's better to burn out than to fade away'. With this quotation from 'Out of the Blue, Into the Black',

Kurt Cobain placed himself directly in the tradition of other rock deaths – Jimi Hendrix, Brian Jones, Sid Vicious. The song had been written in 1978 by Neil Young in despair following the death of Elvis Presley and the rise of punk. Ironically it was exactly by the fusion of punk with seventies rock that Kurt Cobain and Nirvana would transform rock music in the nineties.

The irony would not have escaped him. After all, Kurt would often sign into hotels with Courtney as Mr and Mrs Simon Ritchie, Sid Vicious' real name. However, there could be no irony in the heroin addiction that dogged the last two years of his life and his relationship with Courtney. In the autopsy, 1.52 mg of heroin were found in his blood, three times a fatal dose. On 7 April, before she found out her husband was dead, Courtney Love was rushed to hospital after a suspected overdose and arrested for possession of heroin.

Which is it then? A straightforward rock star drugs death or a tragic figure driven to drugs and eventual suicide by the pressure of fame? Neither provides an adequate explanation of the man and his motivation. For this it is necessary to cast further back to where Kurt was born and what he was trying to escape from.

A Rocky Start

If you take the freeway out of Seattle heading south for California, after fifty miles you see the sign for Route 12, a highway that winds through the mountains past Olympia down to the coast and Aberdeen.

There is little to Aberdeen but trailer parks and logging yards. A drive down main street takes in diners, a five-and-dime, a few bars. Soon enough the town peters out, giving way on one side to endless hillsides of pine and spruce, on the other at the mouth of the Wishkah river, to the Pacific. The highway stops here, a dead-end in a dead-end town. Last stop America, next stop China.

It was here that Kurt Cobain was born on 20 February 1967. His father Donald had a good job as a mechanic at the local Chevron station while his mother Wendy kept home in the house the Cobains bought in Aberdeen six months after Kurt was born.

The neighbourhood was not the best and the family was far from rich, but in Kurt's recollection the period stands out as one of happiness and contentment.

Don fixed up the house, laying wall to wall carpets and putting in wood panelling and a fake fireplace. 'White trash posing as middle class' was how Kurt later described it. His mother was devoted to her first-born son, a love which Kurt remembers: 'My mom was always physically affectionate with me. We always kissed goodbye and hugged. Those were pretty blissful times.' When he was three, a sister Kimberley was added to the Cobain family.

In this stable home environment, Kurt's talents blossomed at an early age. Wendy came from a musical family. Her brother Chuck played in a rock and roll band and her sister Mary played country and western guitar and sang in the bars around Aberdeen. Her uncle Delbert had even recorded ballads in California in the fifties under the name of Dale Arden.

Mary gave Kurt Beatles and Monkees records and when he was seven a bass drum. He used to strap it on and march around the neighbourhood, singing Beatles songs. From third grade, he started having drum lessons. 'Ever since I can remember, since I was a little kid, I wanted to be Ringo Starr. But I wanted to be John Lennon playing drums.' Mary tried to teach him guitar as well but he had no patience.

In fact Kurt was diagnosed as hyperactive. To counteract this, he was prescribed Ritalin, a form of speed. Unfortunately for Kurt this had the effect of keeping him awake until four in the morning. When sedatives were tried instead, he would fall asleep in school.

Despite this, he was an extremely happy child. As Wendy recalls 'He got up every day with such joy that there was another day to be had. He was so enthusiastic. He would come running out of his bedroom so excited that there was another day ahead of him and he couldn't wait to find out what it was going to bring him.'

However, when Kurt was seven, his life was changed and for him an idyllic childhood ended. Don and Wendy's marriage fell apart. Don was barely around, either at work or coaching the high school wrestling and basketball teams. Wendy became increasingly resentful and they began to quarrel. Soon after Kurt's eighth birthday, his parents had separated; by the middle of 1975 they were divorced.

The divorce changed Kurt completely. He became withdrawn and moody. For the first year or so, he stayed with his mother and sister in the family home in Aberdeen. But he took against his mother's new boyfriend, 'a huge mean wife-beater' as far as he was concerned. Wendy put this down to jealousy. Kurt increasingly ran wild and Wendy lost patience and sent him off to live with Don.

After the divorce, Don had got a job with a logging company as a tallyman

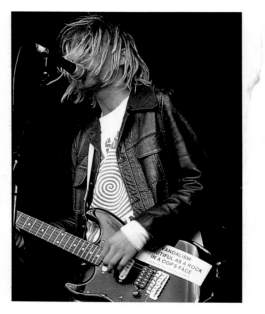

Kurt Cobain

and lived in a trailer in Montesano, twenty miles east of Aberdeen. At first, the move worked well. Don and Kurt would go off for weekends camping in the forest or on the beach. When Don had to work weekends, Kurt would tag along. He would sit for hours on end in his father's van listening to tapes on the 8-track. His favourite was the Queen album 'Message to the World'. He would play the tape until the battery was dead so that when his father came back the van had to be jump started.

However, in 1978 Don remarried and Kurt found himself with a stepmother and a new stepbrother and sister. He felt betrayed and took violently against his stepmother. Kurt began to cut school. At home he refused to do chores and

Kurt Cobain as a child in Aberdeen

picked on his stepbrother. Don's response was to beat him. His father had belted him and he saw no reason to let Kurt get away with anything.

The one refuge for Kurt was in music. His taste by this stage had gone beyond The Beatles and The Monkees. Don had been persuaded by a workmate to join the Colombia House record club. After the first free offer, he soon lost interest but continued to pay the bills. Kurt on the other hand was hooked. Each month another package would come in the mail bringing that month's recommended record, albums by the likes of Aerosmith, Led Zeppelin, Black Sabbath and Kiss. This music went along with the only recognisable counter culture in town. To wear a Kiss t-shirt and fleece-lined denim jacket and to smoke dope through high school was the established way to rebel.

Kurt hung out with the stoners but he knew he did not belong. He was far more inspired by the new movement from England called punk. He never heard any of the music but he would read all he could about it, cutting out articles from *Creem* magazine on Richard Hell, Iggy Pop and the Sex Pistols. He managed to track down one punk record, the Clash album *Sandanista*. When he got it home, he was bitterly disappointed. This was not what punk should sound like.

For his fourteenth birthday, his uncle Chuck made him an offer; he could either have a bike or a guitar. Kurt took the guitar, a secondhand electric that barely played. He took lessons for a week, long enough to learn how to play AC/DC's 'Back in Black'. From this he moved on to working out 'Louie Louie' and 'Another One Bites the Dust'. He wrote his own stuff too, trying to imagine what punk would really be like: 'I tried to play as nasty as I could. Turn my little ten-watt amplifier up as loud as it could go.' His punk introduction was not long in coming.

In Aberdeen, if there were bands, they were cover bands. There was one exception; the Melvins. The Melvins formed around 1981 and were named after a man called Melvin who was arrested for stealing a Christmas tree

from the Montesano Thriftway. Initially
they tried to play like the Ramones –
three-minute songs at 90mph without
too many chord changes. However,
soon the music they were steeped in,
Kiss and Black Sabbath, took hold.
While the rest of the punk world
played super fast, the Melvins got
slower and heavier. As Buzz Osborne,
the lead singer, said 'It was so backward,
it was forward.' Aberdeen was not ready
for punk or the Melvins. When they
played, they never drew a crowd of
more than fifty. All the same, to the
stoner kids, Kurt included, they were
heroes, the closest thing in Aberdeen to
rock stars. Their rehearsals became a
regular hang-out, a social scene for the
town's rebels to smoke dope and listen
to music. Kurt more than most became

devoted to the band, going to every gig and helping with their equipment.

For his part, Buzz turned Kurt on to good music, giving him compilation tapes of southern California punk, bands like Flipper, MDC and the Butt-hole Surfers. Kurt was blown away. 'It was like listening to something from a different planet. It took me a few days to accept it.' Accept it, he swallowed it whole! In August 1984 Black Flag played the Mountaineer Club in Seat-tle. Kurt sold his record collection to get the $12 together for a ticket, driving up to Seattle with the Melvins in their tour van for the gig. He came back, spiked his hair and decided to form a band.

Kurt's sense of a worthwhile vocation was not shared by his parents. He had become sick by now of being passed around from relative to relative, and begged his mother to have him back. In 1984 Wendy had married Pat O'Connor, a long-shoreman with a drink problem. She didn't think she could deal with this as well as Kurt, but she was eventually persuaded to let him come home. Her apprehension was well founded. Kurt spent his time cutting school and smoking dope, arguing with her constantly.

He would spend hours on end in his bedroom, stoned, playing guitar with the amp at full volume. Whenever Wendy went out to work, she would come back to be met by complaints from the neighbours. Soon she lost patience again and told him to go. He went back to live with Don. Don insisted that he give up music and tried to make him join the navy instead. It was no surprise that Kurt lasted in Montesano for a week. After this, he did not see his father again for the next eight years. School was no better. He flunked out in May 1985, six weeks before graduation.

On stage with Nirvana in the early days

The heart of the Grunge scene was in Seattle

All the Ingredients of Grunge

After flunking out of school he got a job (ironically as a caretaker at Aberdeen High) and with a friend rented an apartment in Aberdeen. But then the job became boring, the friend moved out and, months behind with the rent, Kurt was evicted. During the winter of 1985, Kurt survived on $40 of food stamps a month, sleeping rough under the North Aberdeen Bridge. He used the stamps to buy beer and lived off food he could scrounge or fish from the river. He subsequently played the memory down: 'I was just living out the Aberdeen fantasy version of being a punk rocker. It was really easy. It was nothing compared to what most kids are subjected to after they run away to the big city. There was no threat of danger, ever.'

Part of the fantasy was graffiti. He would drink, drop acid and then at night go out and paint the walls around Aberdeen with slogans like 'ABORT CHRIST' and 'GOD IS GAY'. In the end he was arrested by the police, spray can in hand writing 'HOMO SEX RULES' on the side of a bank. Down at the station, they found nothing in his pockets but a guitar pick, a can of beer and a cassette by the punk band Millions of Dead Cops. Kurt was given a $180 fine and thirty-day suspended sentence.

Another part of the fantasy was drugs. He bought from a dealer who got his stock robbing pharmacies. The dealer supplied Kurt with Percodan, a pain-killer derived from opium. Kurt had no idea what they were or that they were addictive but by the summer of 1986 he was taking ten a day and in his own words 'getting real itchy'. After two months, the dealer's supply ran out and Kurt had to go cold turkey. That summer as well he took heroin for the first time, his dealer shooting him up. 'I always wanted to do it – I always knew that I would. It was such a scarce thing to find heroin in Aberdeen that I just thought I would try it.'

Guilty about her son sleeping rough, Wendy helped Kurt out with the deposit for a roof over his head, this time a broken down shack, 1000 1/2 East Second Street. Kurt lived there with Matt Lukin, the Melvins bassist. They had no fridge and only a toaster oven. Neither made any effort to keep the place clean. To make matters worse, Kurt bought six turtles and put them in a bath tub in the middle of the living room. For irrigation he drilled a hole in the floor. Unfortunately the water did not drain but instead started to seep up, rotting the floorboards. There was a constant stench of stagnant water. With this and unpaid rent Kurt was evicted again.

In the meantime he had started going out with Tracy Marander. They met through Buzz Osborne at a punk club in Seattle and when he was evicted he moved in with Tracy in her small studio flat in Olympia.

To earn money, Kurt was desperate enough to start a covers band called the Sellouts to play Creedence Clearwater Revival songs in redneck bars in Aberdeen. In fact, the band never played. Kurt fell out with the bass player who went on to chop his fingers off in a logging accident. However, it marked the first tie-up between Kurt and Chris Novoselic, the six-foot-seven half-Croat with whom Kurt would eventually form Nirvana.

Undeterred by the loss of the bassist (or his fingers), they persevered, getting Aaron Burckhard in to play drums. With this line-up, from late 1987 on, they began to make headway. Kurt had written a strong set of songs – 'Hairspray Queen', 'Spank Thru'', 'Downer' and 'Floyd the Barber' amongst them – and they began to get a following. They had not settled on a name however, playing variously as Skid Row, Throat Oyster, Windowpane. They then tried Bliss (a name Kurt put down to an acid trip) before finally hitting on Nirvana. Kurt and Chris began to believe in what they were doing. Chris and his girlfriend Shelli moved in with Kurt and Tracy in the apartment in Olympia so that the two band members could practice every

Kurt Cobain was a big fan of Sonic Youth

Grunge fashion

night. Kurt even got a job as a caretaker so they could save some money to
make a demo.

Like Spinal Tap, however, they had
drummer trouble. They could not get
Aaron Burckhard out of Aberdeen (he
was not keen on driving the forty miles
to Olympia every night just to practise)
nor Aberdeen out of him (he wanted to
play heavy metal and Led Zep covers in
particular). His unreliability was worst
at the beginning of the month when his
girlfriend's welfare check came in.
They would go out and live it up
with all the other unemployed in
Aberdeen.

When Burckhard was not around, they
played when they could with the

Melvins drummer Dale Crover, but in early 1988 he went off with the rest of the Melvins to live in San Fransisco. Before he went, he recommended Dave Fosterbut, who turned out to be another prime example of Aberdeen man – into heavy metal and fond of a brawl. His time in Nirvana was short-lived, and the band soon found another drummer, Chad Channing. Foster only found out he had been dropped when he saw an advert for a Nirvana gig in the local paper.

Nirvana's sound was not born in a vacuum. While punk left no obvious mark on Seattle, there were some who had been listening and the legacy of grassroots independence and self expression encouraged them, talented or not, to play. Like everywhere else in the States, college radio became keeper of the flame, playing the canon of punk classics on English import and giving air time to local bands. In an attempt to regain the purity of 1977, in the mid-eighties punk went hardcore. This orthodoxy demanded a pared-back, no frills sound and speed-fuelled two-minute songs. Given that punk had never really happened in the Pacific Northwest, its adulteration was never going to be a cause for concern. Instead the ethos was fused with the seventies rock that in Seattle had never really gone away, a style that was christened Grunge.

By January 1988, Kurt and Chris had saved enough to make a demo. They went to Reciprocal Recordings, a broken down studio downtown and home of Jack Endino, house producer for Sub Pop records and as such godfather of the Seattle sound. Endino was a punk believer: he did not produce records, he just recorded them and charged next to nothing for the service. This rough and ready quality became a defining characteristic of Grunge. With Dale Crover on drums, they laid down and mixed ten songs in six hours. The demo cost only $152 but Kurt was happy with the way it turned out.

Endino really liked the tape too. He made a remix and gave a copy to Jonathan Poneman of Sub Pop. At the time Sub Pop were keen to sign new bands to fill out their roster, and Poneman was excited by what he heard.

Nirvana were fresh and from outside the incestuous Seattle scene.

Kurt had not even considered signing for Sub Pop. He wanted to sign for one of the indie labels that his heroes were with: SST in California or Touch & Go in Chicago (home of the Butthole Surfers). He sent off tapes to these but heard no reply. Then Poneman got in touch saying he had heard the tape, liked it and wanted to put out a single. A meeting was arranged at the Café Roma in Seattle. Kurt and Tracy turned up early. Poneman remembers Kurt as being 'very timid and respectful', 'a very nice gentle guy'. Chris arrived late. To calm his nerves, he had been drinking. Throughout the meeting he glared at Poneman breaking in every so often to insult him loudly. Despite Chris' onslaught, a deal was agreed for Sub Pop to put out Nirvana's first record.

The band (by this time Chad Channing was their drummer) went back into the studio with Jack Endino in June 1988. The track selected for the single was 'Love Buzz' , a cover of a song by Shocking Blue, an obscure Dutch psychedelic band from the sixties. However, Sub Pop was over extended and had real cashflow problems. Months passed and still the Nirvana single was not released. Kurt would phone Poneman who would promise again that it would be released soon, until Sub Pop eventually found the money and the record came out in November.

On an Increasing High

Encouraged by the success of the single, Nirvana started rehearsing songs for what was to become their first album, *Bleach*. Sub Pop said they had no money. Despite this, Kurt went ahead and booked a studio with Endino. They started recording on Christmas Eve and by early January had finished the ten tracks. When they went into the studio, Kurt had not finished writing the lyrics. As a result, several of the songs have no more than one verse repeated two or three times. Kurt put this down to expediency. He also claimed that there was nothing personal about the songs. Despite this, many reflect his Aberdeen upbringing.

In 'Swap Meet' Kurt sings about a sight common in parking lots in small-town America, poor people selling what they can secondhand to raise a buck. Kurt described these people as 'white trash entrepreneurs who can't look further than selling junk because they *live* in junk. They're surrounded by it and their whole mentality is based on junk – grease, dirt and poverty.' In other songs he kicked out at his current concerns. 'School' was aimed at the incestuous Seattle scene where it was social death not to listen to the right bands, to hold the right views and be seen with the right people. The chorus 'You're in high school again' is repeated over and over. There was an added irony in making the record sound as much like Grunge was supposed to sound as they could. 'We wrote it about Sub Pop. If we could have thrown in Soundgarden's name, we would have.' Kurt said later, complaining that they had written songs to fit in with what Sub Pop expected of them. At the same time, flashes of Nirvana's future direction came through. 'About the girl' in particular is unashamedly melodic. Tracy had asked Kurt why he didn't write a song about her. This was his response.

The album cost $606 to record. Afterwards Nirvana were due to go on a two-week tour around the North-West, including a gig in San Fransisco. At the time, the city authorities were running a big anti-AIDS campaign encouraging heroin users to 'Bleach their works'. This provided them with the name for the album. Sub Pop released *Bleach* in June 1989. Initial reaction to the album was muted but gradually sales picked up.

They went on their first US tour, all piled in a white van taking turns with the driving. They had no road crew, no one to sort out where they were going to eat or sleep. They played tiny venues and often hardly anyone turned up. But to Kurt the whole thing was an adventure: 'We were totally poor but, God, we

Courtney Love on stage with Hole

A quiet moment

were seeing the United States for the
first time. And we were in a band and we
were making enough money to survive.
It was awesome.' Their poverty was not
helped by their penchant for smashing
equipment, but this quickly became a
Nirvana ritual and a standard part of the
set.

Later in the year they made their first trip
to Europe, touring with another Sub
Pop band, TAD. Starting in New-
castle, they played thirty-six shows in
forty-two days. Most of the time was
spent crammed in a Fiat van driving
between venues. Although they played
to big crowds, the gigs were a strain.
They had to put up with poor equipment, the result of a vicious cycle of
smashing their instruments which they

then had to repair or replace for the next night. Kurt spent most of the tour drunk or asleep. By the time they reached Rome, Kurt was ready to snap, ground down by the tight schedule, the poor food, the cramped bus and poor equipment. Four songs into the set he smashed his guitar, walked off stage and climbed a speaker stack. He threatened to jump before setting off hand over hand across the rafters, screaming at the audience below. He finally reached a balcony from where he was eventually persuaded to come backstage. The band was allowed a few days off after that before completing the tour in London.

As well as playing on his nerves, Kurt's long absences on tour had put a strain on his relationship with Tracy. Halfway through the second US tour in April 1990 Kurt called Tracy from Amherst, Massachusetts, to tell her he was moving out.

When the tour ended, Kurt started to go out with Tobi Vail. Although a couple of years younger than Kurt, Tobi was an impressive figure. She helped start the Riot Grrl movement which through music and fanzines tried to promote feminism in rock (the sexist rock press soon dubbed it Foxcore) and had a definite influence on Kurt's own political thinking. However, the relationship did not last and they split up in November 1990. Kurt, though only twenty-three at the time, wanted more commitment.

Kurt had been writing songs towards their second album. He was moving beyond the formulaic Grunge of *Bleach* to find a blend of a heavy sound with melody. In April 1990 they made a first recording of the new material with Butch Vig at his studio in Wisconsin. The session revealed the shortcomings in Chad's drumming. He could not deliver the big drum sound that Kurt and Chris wanted and sometimes could not play the parts that were written for him. When they came back to Seattle Chad was fired and Nirvana was on the look-out for a drummer again. Soon after this the hardcore band Scream broke up. Kurt and Chris had once seen Scream play and had been impressed by David Grohl the drummer. They invited him up to Seattle to audition. The moment

Alice in Chains, another Seattle band

Nirvana receives an MTV award

they began to play together Kurt and Chris realised that the final piece of the Nirvana sound was in place.

As bootleg copies of the sessions recorded with Butch Vig made the rounds, Nirvana were hotly pursued by the major record labels. They were wined and dined, flown to New York and LA. Having decided to part company with Sub Pop, Nirvana were delighted with the attention. To negotiate the best possible deal, they first signed with a management agency, Gold Mountain who also handled Sonic Youth, long standing heroes of Kurt's, who had become friends of the band. They had come to see the New York show in Nirvana's first US tour in 1989 and in August 1990 asked the band

to support them on a short West Coast
tour. It was no surprise then that they
should influence Nirvana's choice in
persuading them to sign for their label
Geffen. Most of the advance of $287,000
went on taxes, legal fees and to meet
debts. At the same time Geffen paid
$75,000 to Sub Pop to buy the band
out of its contract with them.

The deal with Geffen was not finally
signed until April 1991. Through the
winter the band stayed in Seattle, surviv-
ing on the $1000 a month doled out by
Geffen ahead of their advance. Kurt and
Dave shared the apartment in Olympia,
leaving it only to practise with Chris on
material for the new album. Kurt had
black memories of the period. 'The
whole winter that Dave and I spent

together in that little apartment was the most depressing time I'd had in years. It was so f★★★ing small and dirty and cold and grey every f★★★ing day. I almost went insane at one point. I just couldn't handle it. I was so bored and poor. We were signed to Geffen for months and we didn't have any money. We ended up having to pawn our amps and our TV, all kinds of stuff, just to get money to eat corn dogs. It just felt really weird to be signed to this multimillion-dollar corporation and be totally poor. All we did was practise. It was the only thing that saved us. Even that got repetitious after a while.'

The other consolation Kurt turned to was heroin. Because he spent most of his time asleep during that period, it took a while for anyone to notice. But once on a visit to the Olympia apartment Tracy found him passed out on the bathroom floor, his sleeve rolled up and a spoon in the sink. Chris and Dave made it clear to Kurt what they thought of his drug taking. Kurt did not stop; he just tried to hide his habit.

The Teen Spirit Takes Off

In April 1991, the band went down to
Los Angeles to record the new album
with Butch Vig. The change of climate
and the chance at last to go to work on
the new record brought a change in
mood. Besides Kurt did not know any
dealers in LA so he was off the heroin.
Instead, for an opiate he drank Codeine
cough syrup constantly. The drum and
bass parts were laid down in the first few
days of recording; Kurt was kept longer

doing vocals and guitar overdubs and writing lyrics. Much of the material came from their session the year before with Vig. The arrangements were largely unchanged though many of the lyrics were rewritten. Kurt as usual was self-deprecating about the creative process: 'We downed a lot of hypodermic cough syrup and Jack Daniels and just lounged on the couch in the recreation area of the studio for days on end just writing lyrics here and there.'

Out of this process was born 'Smells Like Teen Spirit'. The song was started from a riff that Kurt hit upon in the studio; the drum and bass parts were built around it. At first it struck them as nothing remarkable. If anything they feared there would be accusations of

Hanging loose

Frances Bean was born on 18 August 1992

ripping off the Pixies in having quiet
verses juxtaposed with loud manic
choruses. However, when the band
heard the playback they knew they
were on to something. The song opens
with a staccato guitar riff, swamped by
the entry of drums, bass and distorted
guitar. A murmured verse follows, tail-
ing off in a sneering 'Hello, Hello,
Hello...'. Then suddenly the chorus
erupts with Kurt screaming almost un-
intelligibly 'With the lights out, its less
dangerous/Here we are now entertain
us/I feel stupid and contagious/Here we
are now entertain us/A mulatto, an
albino, a mosquito, my libido'. On the
page the lyrics make little sense, but set
against the raw emotion of the music the
whole somehow comes together. As
Kurt saw it, the song was about his

audience and the band in relation to that audience. With a title 'Smells Like Teen Spirit' and an opening line of 'Load up on guns and bring your friends' it is a song of revolution, a call to arms. On the other hand Kurt was reacting to the pressure on him to be some sort of political spokesman; he sings 'I found it hard, it was hard to find/Oh well whatever never mind ' and ends up repeating over and over 'a denial, a denial'. In other words it may smell *like* teen spirit but it is not the real thing. The fact that Teen Spirit is a brand of deodorant adds to this sarcasm.

Kurt addressed the ambivalent relation-ship he had with his audience again on the next track, 'In Bloom'. The chorus hits out at the rock fans that the band was beginning to attract who had little sympathy with Kurt's punk roots: 'He's the one who likes all the pretty songs/And he likes to sing along/And he likes to shoot his gun/But he knows not what it means'. The irony is that the tune is so good that it is hard not to sing along.

The rest of the album hits similar heights, the range and intensity of Kurt's writing showing how much his style had developed since Bleach.

When *Nevermind* was finished, everyone was pleased with the result. They knew it was good; though they wouldn't find out until 'Smells Like Teen Spirit' was released in September exactly how good. As a result the summer of 1991 found them optimistic and full of confidence. They toured Europe supporting Sonic Youth, playing the Reading Festival. Kurt summed it up: 'The most exciting time for a band is right before they become really popular. I'd love to be in bands that just do that every two years. Every time I look back at the best times in this band it was right before Nevermind came out. It was awesome.'

Kurt had another reason for feeling good. He started to see Courtney Love. They had in fact met two years before at a gig in Portland, Oregon. Nirvana were playing support for another band. Courtney recalled Kurt as 'hot in a Sub Pop rock god sort of way' while Kurt remembered 'She looked like Nancy Spungen . . . a classic punk rock chick.' The comparison had not escaped others. Nancy Spungen was the girlfriend of Sid Vicious. Already a well-known punk groupie, she became the first lady of punk and their stormy relationship was followed with all the attention of a royal marriage. She introduced him to heroin and their lives took a downward spiral that ended when Spungen was found stabbed to death in their suite at the Chelsea Hotel and Sid Vicious, after two months in Rykers Island, overdosed while on bail charged with her murder.

Courtney had an almost mythical past. Daughter of Grateful Dead roadie Hank Harrison, at the age of three she appeared on the back of the Dead's *Aoxomoxoa* album. Later, after her parents split up,

her mother took her from LA to New
Zealand, to Australia and then back to the
States where Courtney wound up in an
Oregon reform school. During her teens,
she supported herself as a stripper, travel-
ling from Portland to Japan and Ireland.
By 1981 she was in Liverpool, hanging
out with Echo and the Bunnymen and
Julian Cope. She then moved back to the
States where she sang in a succession of
bands in between landing parts as a movie
actress, in Sid and Nancy and then Straight
to Hell which featured the Pogues, Joe
Strummer and Elvis Costello. In 1990 she
founded her own band, Hole.

There was no doubt from the first
meeting that the two were attracted.
She was friends with Dave Grohl and
confessed to him her feelings for Kurt.

Kurt Cobain never wanted to be a superstar

With Courtney Love and Frances Bean

Through him she sent Kurt a heart-shaped box filled with sea shells, pine cones and miniature tea cups. They met again in May 1991 at a Butthole Surfers gig. As a greeting Courtney punched Kurt in the stomach. He punched her back, then he leaped on her and they began to wrestle. According to Courtney 'It was a mating ritual for dysfunctional people'. During the recording of *Nevermind* she dropped by the recording studio a few times. Afterwards when he was away on tour in Europe she would call him, though she was going out with Billy Corgan, lead singer of the Smashing Pumpkins, at the time.

Nevermind was released, with 'Smells Like Teen Spirit' as the first single, in September 1991. No one was prepared for the impact it would have. On the stations for alternative music, the song quickly became an anthem. WOZQ, the college station in New England, once played the record sixty-seven times in a single week (including once on a reggae show). More importantly, MTV picked up on the video. It appeared first in their Buzz Bin, but the audience reaction was so positive that soon they played the video five or six times a day. *Nevermind* opened at 144 on the Billboard chart; by December it had reached number one, selling over 300,000 copies a week. *Alternative Press* best captured the mood: 'In September 1991 Nirvana were just a local cult, the latest alternative morsel to drop down Geffen's gullet. By October they were U2 and Springsteen, Presley and the Pistols rolled into one snarling bundle.'

Love and Destruction

Their lives were transformed. That autumn, touring the States to promote the album, they found their audience increasingly made up of heavy metal kids and Guns n' Roses fans. The change did not agree with Kurt. 'I found myself being overly obnoxious during the *Nevermind* tour because I noticed that there were more average people coming into our shows and I didn't want them there. They started to get on my nerves.'

To compensate they stepped up the guitar-smashing. 'We were feeling so weird because we were being treated like kings so we had to destroy everything.'

After the US tour they went back to Europe. Kurt was disillusioned and soon was bored of touring. So he turned to Courtney – Hole were on tour in Europe at the same time – and they renewed their telephone romance. Courtney skipped on a Hole show just so she could visit Kurt in Amsterdam. Kurt too began to slip up on his band schedule.

For further excitement that time in Amsterdam Kurt and Courtney turned to heroin. Kurt insisted that it was his

Kurt Cobain was found dead at his home outside Seattle

Fans gather after Cobain's death to celebrate the Teen Spirit idea. In December, when the Nirvana tour ended, Kurt went back to Seattle. Courtney was still in Europe with Hole. Kurt began to do heroin daily. He said he needed the drug to ease the pain that he had in his stomach, a chronic condition that successive doctors were unable to diagnose or treat. When Courtney flew back from London, he went down to LA to be with her. The couple went from hotel to hotel, doing what Courtney called 'bad Mexican LA heroin'.

When just after Christmas Nirvana went off on a short tour supporting the Chili Peppers, Dave and Chris noticed that something was wrong. It was not lost on the press either. The January edition of *BAM* magazine noted that Kurt was 'nodding off in mid-sentence', adding that 'the pinned pupils, sunken cheeks and scabbed sallow skin suggest something more serious than fatigue.' It was in this state that Kurt went to New York to appear on 'Saturday Night Live'. Kurt and Courtney made all the necessary preparations, taking a junkie friend of theirs along to score for them. Kurt's drug use was putting a strain on the band. His moods were erratic, his behaviour unreliable. Chris and Dave saw less and less of Kurt, though the band was meant to be going on a tour of Australia and New Zealand at the end of the month.

More importantly, it was at this time that Courtney discovered she was pregnant. She claims that she stopped taking heroin straightaway and went to a specialist

for a full medical check to ensure the
baby would be all right. Kurt too tried to
clean up, going into a detox centre. But
once on tour, his stomach played up
again and he was prescribed physeptone, a kind of methadone.

The tour ended in Hawaii. Kurt and
Courtney had decided the time was
right to be married. The ceremony
took place on a cliff above a beach on
24 February 1992. Kurt had run out of
physeptone and had to persuade a fried
to bring him some heroin as a wedding
present. There were only a handful of
people there including Dave but not
Chris. Chris' wife Shelli had been more
outspoken in blaming Courtney for
what had happened to Kurt. Kurt refused to invite her to the wedding so

Chris decided that if his wife was not invited he would not go either.

This estrangement increased after the tour and Chris and Kurt did not talk for about five months. While Chris and Dave went back to Seattle, Kurt and Courtney moved into an apartment in LA, where Kurt began his daily round of shooting up again. He worked his way up to a $400 a day habit, the maximum his cash machine would give him in a day. The group came close to splitting up not only because of the drugs but because Kurt demanded a redistribution of the royalties from Nevermind. To that point they had been split evenly but Kurt insisted that as songwriter he should be given the lion's share. He demanded seventy-five per cent of all royalties retroactively. Chris and Dave eventually gave in but for a long time afterwards the bitterness remained.

From the beginning of the year the press had begun to scent a possible story in Kurt and Courtney as drug addicts. In June Nirvana had to go back to Europe to play some gigs they had skipped the autumn before. The day after the Belfast show, Kurt collapsed and had to be rushed to hospital. The rumour went round that he had overdosed, the record label insisted that it was exhaustion. In fact Kurt had forgotten to take his methadone the night before. Despite the fact that he had been on heroin continuously for the preceding six months, questions about drug abuse were still met with flat denials.

All this was in vain however when the September edition of *Vanity Fair* hit the newsstands carrying an interview with Courtney by Lynn Hirschberg. Hirschberg portrayed Courtney as a 'a charismatic opportunist and proud of it', with a 'train-wreck personality'. Buried in the later paragraphs of the piece were details of her drug binge with Kurt in New York and the apparent admission that she had taken heroin when she knew she was pregnant. Immediately they were besieged by the press and took refuge by checking into hospital. Courtney was close to confinement in any case and Kurt wanted to make an attempt to go clean. Gold Mountain tried to minimise the damage, claiming that the pair had only had a brief experimentation with heroin. But the world was convinced that the pair were junkies and that Courtney's baby would be deformed. In this they were disappointed and on 18 August Frances Bean was born healthy and completely normal. However, on the back of the *Vanity Fair* piece the LA County Department of Child Services moved in. Kurt and Courtney were forced to surrender custody of Frances Bean to Courtney's sister. For a month afterwards they were not allowed to be alone with their daughter.

It was no surprise that their relations with the press were hostile after this episode, and Kurt gave an effective reply on stage when, a week after Frances' birth, Nirvana headlined at the Reading Festival. Kurt came on in a wheelchair and wearing a hospital gown, sending up press reports regarding his health. Two weeks later they were scheduled to appear at the MTV Music Awards. Kurt wanted to play a new song, 'Rape Me', and it was no surprise that MTV refused. It looked as if Nirvana would not appear despite the fact that *Nevermind* was expected to win in a number of categories. At the last minute, Kurt relented and agreed to play 'Lithium'. The appearance went a long way to dispel rumours about his addiction. By the end of the year they had managed to persuade the authorities that Frances should be allowed to live with them, though they had to go through the indignity of regular urine tests.

Meanwhile, Kurt was preparing songs for a new album. It was now eighteen months since they had finished recording Nevermind and the time was right for another album.

By this stage Grunge had become mainstream. The charts were dominated by the Seattle sound, with bands like Soundgarden, Alice in Chains and Pearl Jam. In the process, Grunge had lost its edge and its threat to the establishment. It had even taken to the catwalks, with the December issue of *Vogue* filled with Grunge fashion. This dismayed Kurt. He was determined to make a record that would challenge the audience gathered from *Nevermind*. To this end Steve Albini was chosen as producer. It seemed a strange choice given that

Albini was known to hold the opinion that Nirvana were unremarkable, 'R.E.M. with a fuzzbox' as he put it. However to Kurt he was a legend. Not only had he produced for one of Kurt's favourite bands, the Pixies, but he had played with Big Black, a hugely influential Chicago punk group of the early eighties.

In February 1993, they went to Albini's studio in Minnesota. They recorded everything within about six days. Most tracks were recorded live with only the minimum of retakes or changes. When the results were handed over to the management at Geffen they hated it. Kurt was unapologetic, but when he returned from Minnesota he began to have doubts. The bass sound was muddy and the whole seemed to lack finish. It was agreed that some of the tracks should be remixed. Meanwhile Albini gave an interview to the *Chicago Tribune* alleging that Geffen would not release the record. This theme was taken up by *Newsweek* which reported the rumour that the record was unreleasable. In the end only two tracks – 'Heart-shaped Box' and 'All Apologies'– were significantly changed. Kurt worked on the remixes with Scott Litt, the producer of R.E.M. in Seattle in May.

Taking the Blame

When *In Utero* was finally released in September, it may have come as a surprise how listenable the album was, despite the harder edge to the sound. But this could not hide the bitterness and rage in the lyrics, as Kurt took his chance to have his say on the events since *Nevermind*. From the start Kurt laid out his scorn for his fans: 'Teenage angst has paid off well/Now I'm bored and old'; the record company and rock press: 'Self appointed judges judge/More than they have sold'; critics of Courtney: 'If she floats then she is not/A witch like we had thought'; and how he and his music were reduced to the product of a broken home: 'Serve the servants – oh no/That legendary divorce is such a bore'. The fans are mocked again when the third song opens with what is recognisable as the guitar riff from 'Smells Like Teen Spirit' over which Kurt screams 'Rape me /Rape me , my friend.' Where the songs are not enraged, Kurt exhibits a weary acceptance, in particular on 'All apologies' which ends the album with Kurt sounding tired and defeated; 'What else should I be/All apologies' and 'Everything is my fault/I'll take all the blame'.

While the record did not create the same
hysterical reaction that had followed the
release of *Nevermind*, in a way it did not
need to. Nirvana were now thoroughly
established MTV darlings and the per-
ceived standard bearers of the indie
scene. There were no surprises: the
interviews, reviews and videos went
ahead as they might have done for
Guns 'n Roses or the Rolling Stones;
their tour to promote the album sold out
everywhere before they played a note.
Kurt could not escape; he had become
the kind of rock star he could not stand.

His music still provided a way out to
break the ennui. In July 1993 at the New
Music Seminar in New York he played
an acoustic set. The audience was dismayed, booing and shouting out at him

to play some rock music. He followed this in October by appearing in the MTV 'Unplugged' series. Again the audience were puzzled: there was no 'Smells Like Teen Spirit' but instead covers of old Vaselines numbers and 'The man who sold the world' by David Bowie. There was a sense of huge potential, that he could turn his hand to anything. Instead what his audience wanted and what Geffen were intent to give them was Nirvana.

All that October and November, they toured the States. The band were playing well, having added a second guitarist, Pat Smear, to the line-up. Kurt too was in good form, off heroin since May. However the tour involved long periods of separation from Courtney and

Frances Bean and he was frequently remote and abstracted. After Christmas the tour moved to Europe. On Kurt's wishes, Nirvana were supported in London by the legendary punk band The Raincoats and in France by The Buzzcocks. All went well until the end of February but then Kurt just seemed to come to a halt. He played badly in Milan and again in Germany. Finally after a concert on 1 March in Munich, he declared he had had enough and would not play again.

He flew down to Rome and checked into the Excelsior Hotel where Courtney and Frances flew in from London to meet him. But this was not enough to lift his mood. It is not clear what happened, whether they quarrelled and about what, but on 3 March Kurt made his first suicide attempt, washing 50 Rohypnol pills down with champagne. Courtney came back the next morning to find him in a coma, a suicide note by his body. Kurt was rushed to hospital where after a couple of days he made a full recovery. Gold Mountain passed the overdose off as accidental over-indulgence; Courtney put it down to a quarrel: 'If he thinks he can get away from me like that he can forget it. I'll follow him through hell.' Kurt said nothing.

The couple returned to Seattle on 10 March. On the surface everything was fine. According to the record company, when Kurt had recuperated Nirvana would play the dates that had been cancelled at the end of the European

tour. In fact, Kurt was hurtling towards
self-destruction at an accelerating pace.
Straightaway he was sighted again in his
old heroin haunts, Denny Way and
Viretta Park. Courtney feared that if
his drug problem were made public
they would lose Frances again. She
organised an intervention, gathering
friends and family to confront him with
his problem and their disapproval.
Threatened with divorce by Courtney,
he joined her in a 12-step rehabilitation
programme in a hospital in Marina Del
Rey, California. He lasted three days
before, without saying anything to
Courtney, he discharged himself and
went back to Seattle. He bought a
shotgun, claiming he needed it for
self-defence, and then disappeared.

Courtney had no idea where he was. For three days she looked for him in LA and hired private detectives to search Seattle. As time passed she grew desperate. She rang all his friends and his mother who in turn reported him missing to the Seattle Police. It was too late.

On 5 April Kurt returned to his mansion in Lake Washington Boulevard. He shot up with heroin and valium, put the shotgun in his mouth and squeezed the trigger with his toe. He was twenty-seven.

It is easy to say that Kurt Cobain died too young. What is harder to see is how he would have lived any longer and kept his sense of integrity. Being the product of a punk tradition had a high price. He wanted to be an outcast, an irritant, to be heard and understood by only a small community of believers that shared his punk ideals. Instead, Nirvana had become a bloated rock event as bankrupt, as he saw it, as any of the bands he had come to destroy. Nirvana's arrival in 1991 may have answered a need for a return to something raw and vital, but Nirvana's staying saw them reduced to a convenient cipher for the slacker generation, a template for major labels and a circus for the media. He loathed himself and despised those around him. In his songs he had taunted his audience from the beginning; despite his scorn they kept listening. In his rock star death of drugs and suicide he taunted them again; there would be nothing more to listen to.